The **50**
Best Games for
**Children's**
**Groups**

**The 50 Best Group Games Pocket Books**

# The **50**
# Best Games for
# **Children's**
# **Groups**

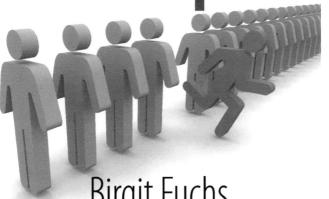

Birgit Fuchs
translated by Lilo Seelos

HINTON**HOUSE**

Published in 2009 by

**Hinton House Publishers Ltd**
Newman House, 4 High Street,
Buckingham, MK18 1NT, UK

info@hintonpublishers.com
www.hintonpublishers.com

**British Library Cataloguing in Publication Data**
Birgit Fuchs
The 50 best games for children's groups. – (The 50 best group games pocket
books ; 6)
1. Group games
I. Title II. Series III. The fifty best games for children's groups
790.1'922-dc22

ISBN-13: 9781906531126

Originally published in German by Don Bosco
Verlag München under the title *Die 50 besten
Spiele für Kindergruppen*
© Don Bosco Verlag, München 2007

Contents

**Contents**

'A person is only human
where he plays.'

*– Friedrich Schiller*

# Grumpy Frog

Ask one player to sit in the middle of the circle and challenge them to answer all questions posed by the other players with a sulky and grumpy 'No'. Players could ask, for example, 'Would you like a lollipop?', 'No', shouts the grumpy frog and looks around angrily. 'Would you like to go deep-sea diving with Flipper?' 'Do you fancy a trip to the cinema?', and so on.

Questions are likely to become more and more ridiculous and, where possible, those asking questions should try to accompany them with exaggerated gestures, funny faces or silly noises. It will be impossible for the grumpy frog to remain in a bad mood.

The group have achieved their goal when the grumpy frog can no longer keep from laughing. The frog is allowed to choose a new grumpy frog, whose mood will be put to the test in turn.

# ... Lives Here

If there is a group of people behind a closed door, who call themselves 'Mrs Fletcher's Class' or 'Music and Drama Group' or 'Scout Troop A', no one actually knows that someone called Jason might be part of the group.

Therefore, get the group to make a large door sign, listing the names of every group member, even the youngest and newest. After all, every member of the group is equally important, which (hopefully) even the youngest of children already know.

To make doubly sure that no one is overlooked, a second notice can be made to go underneath the door sign: A piece of coloured card on which each group member has left a foot print showing that this group stands together.

## Materials

- ☼ coloured card
- ☼ colouring pens
- ☼ finger paint

# Name Pictures

Have you experienced something like this? It is a child's first day at school and they are asked what their name is. They answer 'Sweetie' Johnson and everyone laughs.

To save children from this kind of embarrassment, it is worth paying attention to and deliberately addressing children by their correct first names, as names are closely linked with people's identity.

The following game is all about developing and creating positive associations with people's names.

Each person is given strips of paper and colouring pens. They must now write their first names in large printed letters on their strips of paper, leaving space after each letter. Help any younger children write their names if they are not able to do this on their own.

Now the thinking part of the game starts. Everyone has to come up with a little picture for each letter of their first name, somehow incorporating the shape of the letter into each picture.

The completed artwork can be put together to make a group poster or hung on the child's bedroom door.

## Materials

☀ paper

☀ colouring pens

# Flower King & Flower Queen

Flowers often have noble or interesting names such as Lily of the Valley, Bird of Paradise, Bishop's Hat, Queen Ann's Lace, and so on. Discuss different names with the group and encourage them to think of a name for an imaginary flower.

For this game, each group member is given a flower bulb to plant into a pot of compost. Attach a sign to each pot showing the name of the planter as well as their made-up flower name.

Everyone can choose a sunny spot on the window sill for their bulb and must be responsible for caring for it on a daily basis. Encourage group members to imagine that they are the bulb or flower – what kind of treatment would they be looking for? What kind of end result could be achieved with good care?

This flower game can be an exciting activity, especially when group members link the topics discussed back to themselves: What sort of care would I need myself, what kind of treatment would be good for me, what sort of regular 'pampering' sessions would help me perform best?

## Tip

Amaryllis bulbs are particularly suitable, because they tend to shoot several flowers of huge dimensions.

## Materials

☼ flower pots      ☼ compost

☼ flower bulbs      ☼ paper

☼ pens

# Tina-Burger & Nina-Noodle

Everybody has a favourite dish.

For example, Tina's mouth waters at the thought of fish burgers. However, these have to consist of exactly two fish fingers and some lettuce sandwiched within a roll and cemented together with lots of mayonnaise.

Nina, on the other hand, prefers a special type of curly pasta in cheese sauce with a dollop of ketchup on top! Different people have different tastes.

Group members can have fun by trying to link peoples' names directly to their favourite delicious meal. People are likely to remember dishes named after them for a long time.

Enjoy your meal!

## Tip

Such special dishes can also be named after whole groups or families.

# Lion, Bird, Mouse

For this game, the group leader needs to prepare about ten questions, which the children do not necessarily have to be able to answer. What they should be able to do is to choose from three multiple-choice answers and indicate their choice by marking a box with a circle. Funny questions should definitely be given preference! Prepare the question sheets and hand out to the group.

The leader starts by reading out the first question from their sheet. The children's sheet shows only the three answers with three boxes to be marked with a circle. Each column is assigned an animal symbol. Who is likely to be correct: the bird, the mouse or the lion?

## Game board

*Example:*
Question 1: What do you call a baby deer?

Question 2 + 3 answer choices

Question 3 … and so on

| | | |
|---|---|---|
| Zawn | Fawn | Dawn |
|  |  |  |
|  |  |  |

Each round consists of three children taking part at the same time and using one answer sheet. They sit together in front of the game board and listen to the first question: 'What do you call a baby deer?'

Allow about a minute of thinking time, before uncovering the answer sheet. Is the baby deer called a 'zawn', a 'fawn', or a 'dawn'?

This may well be tricky for the children to decide, in which case, all they can do is quickly choose an answer by circling one of the boxes, regardless of what their two neighbours decide. Who knows whether they actually know the correct answer!

Each child uses a different colour to mark their choice. The leader then uses a highlighter to circle the correct answer. This way it will be easy to see at the end of the game how many correct answers each player has made.

## Tip

Think about why Tony and his friend Henry have always marked the same (wrong) box with a circle. Could it be that neither of them dares to have their own opinion?

# Largometer Pictures

It can seem quite unfair to be in the youngest class, or to be the smallest in a group and to keep being told to 'Wait until you are bigger!'.

So, what would happen if the little members of the group all of a sudden turn into tall beanpoles, who can appear to have greater influence and authority? How would they feel?

Nothing could be easier. On a hot summer's day, take the smallest of the group out into the sunshine, where they are likely to throw shadows of huge dimensions onto the ground. Quickly get some chalk and draw around their shadows. Finally, have fun measuring these giant outlines.

## Tip

If you like, you can place a large piece of paper on the floor and draw the shadow picture onto the paper for the children to keep and use as a motivator on low days.

# Open-End

In this activity the group will need to make decisions and think in a structured and tactical way to find a conclusion to a story with no ending.

It doesn't matter whether or not everyone in the group can write as the task is actually to draw the ending of the story.

For this activity, the leader needs to select a picture book from the library, appropriate to the ability of the group. Picture books with a clear ending are particularly appropriate.

Sit in a circle with the group and read and discuss the story right up to the ending (you could use a big book or show individual pictures on a projector or white board). Now discuss with the group what might happen next and get them to draw their ideas.

Creativity and courage are required for this part of the exercise. Group members need to recognise that even if they think their idea for the ending is not very exciting, or even a little strange, the rest of the group might actually decide that it is the best one.

# The Sun Rises

All members of the group lie down on the floor, pretending to be asleep. They are allowed to peep, otherwise no one will notice the sun rising.

The sun appears in form of a large, yellow cardboard disc, which the group leader or a chosen player has hidden behind their back. When that person lets the yellow sun rise up to the sky (by slowly holding it up), it is the signal for the 'sleeping' players to wake up. Quickly they get up from their sleeping places and move freely around the room. While they are moving around, they must keep an eye on the sun, because as soon as the sun goes down again, they must lie down and go back to sleep.

In this activity the player who is controlling the sun has special power over the others. They can put the others in motion or stop them in their tracks at will.

## Materials

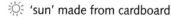 'sun' made from cardboard

# Little Dot & Friends

This fun game is particularly suitable for playing on summer days, when participants are not wearing many layers of clothing, with long sleeves, trousers or tights. Using a biro each player hides five little dots somewhere on their body, for example, on their ear lobe, behind their elbow, on their knee, on their shoulder and on their other arm. Dots should not be on the face or on body parts usually covered with clothing!

Once prepared, one body painter at the time presents themselves to a partner or the whole group, whose task it is to find the five little dots as quickly as possible.

## Tip

You could use a stop watch to determine the quickest dot detectives.

# Quick Check

Divide the group into pairs and one pair at a time, ask the partners to stand opposite each other, eye to eye. Now give them about one minute to study each other and try to remember as many details as possible about the other's appearance.

Now the rest of the group put the pair's observational skills and memory to the test. Both players must turn through 180° and stand back to back. The group have the task of thinking up questions to ask the two players.

☼ Do they remember the pattern and colour of their partner's socks?

☼ Did the trousers have a black and blue or black and green pattern?

☼ Were earrings worn, and if so, what colour were they?

One observation point is given for each correct answer.

## Rule

Both players are asked the same number of questions. In addition, each player is allowed one 'Quick Check Joker', which they can decide to use before they answer a question and which is worth ten points if they answer the question correctly.

# Group Stew

Ask the group to imagine that together they make a complete dish and that the individual group members are the ingredients for this delicious recipe.

Now ask each person to write down on a piece of paper the proportions of the individual members that are added to the recipe.

For example, Anna might write:

*Blue Group Recipe*
1 kg James
½ kg Amy
½ kg Ben
100g Anna

Anna's recipe is then compared to someone else's, for example, Ben's:

*Blue Group Recipe*
1 kg Amy
1 kg Anna
100g James
100g Ben

How interesting! Anna appears to see herself as the weakest member, but so does Ben. What about Amy and James' recipes? It might be time to get together as a group and think about why this is, and for how long and how often they feel this way.

# Caterpillar Wave

Ask all of the group to lie down on the floor in a chain, with their heads on the tummy of the person in front them.

Now the first person in the chain tenses their stomach muscles to lift the head of the next person who is resting on their tummy. As soon as that person feels their head being lifted, they must tighten their own stomach muscles to pass the movement on to the next player and so on, producing a wave like a caterpillar moving along a leaf.

## Tip

A particularly funny variation of this activity is the caterpillar laugh. Instead of the straight-forward tummy wave, the children pass on a happy laugh, until the whole group is lying on the floor laughing.

# Picture an Animal

Give each group member a paper and pen. Then give them the following instructions:

☀ Imagine you are an animal.

☀ Imagine your neighbour is an animal.

☀ Imagine everyone in the group has turned into an animal.

☀ Which animal would suit which person?

Draw a picture of our group as an animal family and label individual animals with corresponding group members' names.

Now all group members start drawing, making sure they don't forget anybody and including members that are absent.

Afterwards, the group can get together to discuss the pictures, providing all artists with the opportunity to explain their animal choices:

Tim as a shark – who would have thought it? Sharks are unpredictable, strong animals, so why has Brian drawn Tim as a shark and what might that tell us about Brian?

All this can be discussed within the group. This activity can be very intriguing, for example, when looking at someone else's animal family, Tim might find himself being portrayed as a rabbit, a little rabbit that would not harm a fly ...

# Clap-Wham-Bang

For this game, the group leader will need to get hold of at least as many paper bags as there are group members, these can be obtained from a bakery or grocer's shop.

Give one bag to each person in the group and then ask all group members to sit in a circle and blow up their paper bags. Ask people to scrunch together the top of their bags to prevent the air from escaping too soon.

Now everyone must raise their free hand in preparation for hitting their paper bag. They must all freeze in this position until it is their turn. The first group member pops their bag and as soon as the sound of the bang has faded, the person next to them pops their bag, which, in turn, is the signal for the next person, and so on.

In this way, group members create a chain reaction of bangs. This exercise requires good concentration and turn-taking skills in order to create the best chain reaction.

# It's Me

This game of 'Tag' requires group members to recognise each other by the sound of their voices.

One person – the Catcher – stands facing the wall. The rest of the group stand behind the Catcher and stay very still and quiet. Using only gestures, they agree on one speaker at a time.

The speaker then taps the Catcher's back three times and the Catcher, without turning round, responds by asking, 'Who's there?' The tapper responds with only one word, 'Me!'

Can the Catcher recognise who has tapped their back? If not, they can ask twice more, but only receive the same short answer each time. As soon as the Catcher has guessed the name of the person who has tapped them on the back, that person has to run off immediately with the Catcher chasing after them. Once the tapper has been caught, they become the Catcher for the next round.

# Friendship Boxes

Friendship boxes can be created very easily and bring great pleasure to people of all ages.

To make a friendship box, you need to get an empty matchbox and cover it in some coloured paper. You can also decorate your box using glitter, beads or natural materials.

Now you need to think about what might fit inside your little box. This could be anything that you think your friend might like. You could put in real objects such as three jelly babies for someone with a sweet tooth, a glass marble for a person who loves playing marbles, a painted pebble for a friend who is interested in mystical things or a feather for someone interested in nature.

However, friendship boxes are really meant to have symbolic contents. Group members could look through catalogues or magazines for pictures or symbols representing what they would like to give their friend, cut them out and put them inside the box.

Such coded secret symbols could, for example, mean:

☼ I would like to go on an outing with you.

☼ I am inviting you for supper.

☼ Thank you for lending me your favourite comic.

The receiver of the message, which is meant for them alone, is likely to be able to interpret it correctly.

## Materials

☼ One empty matchbox per person

☼ Wrapping paper

☼ Beads

☼ Glitter

# Emergency Signals

This game requires group members to recognise non-verbal signals. To start with, everyone strolls around the room as if they are going for a little walk.

Before starting the walk, give one person a piece of paper outlining their fate. During their walk, they might have to, for example:

☀ pretend to faint

☀ pretend to trip and wrench their ankle

☀ pretend to have a heart attack while jogging

While everyone else is happily walking around the room chatting to each other, the main player needs thinks about what kind of emergency signals they will send out. They should consider that, often, emergencies happen quietly and without anyone noticing.

☀ Who will be first to notice that there is a person who needs help or appears to be in real danger?

☀ How do we react appropriately in emergency situations?

☀ How can bystanders work together to manage the situation?

Obviously, this game cannot pre-empt a real emergency, but can help to make group members more observant and aware of possible situations where they may need to recognise what is going on and act quickly and appropriately.

# Saucepan & Lid

To prepare for this hunt-the-partner game, you will need to note down on slips of paper pairs of objects that go together logically. You will need half as many pairs as you have group members.

☀ pencil – eraser

☀ trousers – belt

☀ saucepan – lid

☀ cork – bottle

☀ bicycle - bell

☀ apple – apple crumble

Now divide your group into two. Players in the first half are each given the name of an object from one column, then the names of the other objects are shared out among the second half of the group.

Names should be given out without people seeing what everyone else has been given. Next, everyone should walk around the room and ask each other questions relating to their objects – without giving away the name, for example, 'I have got something that you write with. Have you got anything that goes with that?'

Pairs who have found each other can sit down and watch the others looking for their own partners.

# Dodge-Ball Soft-Ball

Played under the right conditions, dodge ball is a much better game than it is generally given credit for. All too often, it is thought of only as an aggressive game.

However, approaching situations with confidence is an ability that is very desirable in life. In fact, without this skill, people would lose the ability to confidently tackle difficult situations. So why not build the ability to face up to attacks, to be able to go on the attack yourself and to develop clever avoidance strategies!

'Dodge-ball Soft-Ball' is the perfect solution. The ball is soft and players won't have to hide because they are worried about being hurt. This way they will learn to deliberately overcome their fear and look 'danger' in the eye. In addition, the game is particularly good at reducing feelings of aggression!

# Sock Marbles

We all know the feeling - you are really cross or frustrated, but can only vent this verbally, even though what you really want to do vent it physically!

For this game, hitting something isn't just allowed it is actually a requirement!

Two players sit opposite each other, leaving some distance between them and roll a glass marble backwards and forwards between each other as quickly as possible. Both players are 'armed' with a 'hitting sock'. A 'hitting sock' is simply a normal sock into which a second sock has been stuffed. Once armed with a sock, players simply have to wait for the marble to whiz past and than whack it as hard as possible with the sock.

One anger point is given for each hit. Knock your socks off!

## Tip

If there are several angry 'sock hit men' sitting along the track, they can swap places after five marbles have passed to ensure everyone has an equal chance of hitting a marble.

# Washing Away Anger

Why not introduce a ritual where a person who is annoyed 'washes the hair' of the person who is the source of their annoyance. This could be a normal hair wash or a scalp massage.

During this enjoyable process, only the 'hair dresser' is allowed to voice their pent-up frustration, although this should be within reason and the massage should be gentle and kindly. They are only allowed to vent their anger for as long as it takes to wash the other person's hair/give them a head massage. The person who is receiving the massage must listen silently – and enjoy the treatment!

Being treated in a gentle and kindly manner will make it easier to deal with any kind of criticism. And perhaps the remains of any residual annoyance between the two will be flushed down the drain with the final rinse.

# Bottom-Softball

Instead of smacking someone's bottom to give them an old-fashioned and inappropriate punishment, this game is about smacking bottoms while laughing as much as possible.

All group members, regardless of whether they feel angry or not, must stand in a line, lean forward and rest their hands on their upper thighs.

Behind them at a distance of about three metres stands the first 'bottom marksman', armed with a very soft ball.

At a signal, the 'marksman' tries to hit the sticking out bottom of each of the lined-up members and is rewarded with one point for each hit. To release more frustrations, the marksman can give a reason why each person might deserve a smack on the bottom!

## Materials

☼ a soft ball

# Attack of the Wolves

For this game you will need to prepare sticky labels with two different symbols, one representing a wolf - for example, a red tooth - and the other representing a sheep - for example, a yellow circle. There should be enough sticky labels for everyone in the group to choose one each and there should be an equal number of wolves and sheep.

Get the players to select one label each from a bag and ask someone else to help them stick their label on their back.

Then the sheep start moving about without a care in the world. Players should try to imitate both the movements associated with sheep, for example, rather hesitant, small steps, fearful, needing to be with a herd, clumsy ...

As soon as an agreed signal is given, the wolves start to attack. They are powerful and agile in the pursuit of their victims, they snarl, growl, howl and threaten, but without actually touching any of the sheep.

Animals from both groups have to try and pull the sticky label off each other's backs when they are not paying attention. If they manage to do this, the two players swap animal roles. Otherwise, roles are swapped at a five-minute whistle blow.

# Kissing Chain

This game is a good one to play within families, but if playing with children who don't know each other very well, make sure no-one feels pressured to take part.

Sit in a circle on the floor. Players take turns to start a round. The person who is going to start thinks of a place on the face that they would like to honour with a kiss, for example, the tip of the nose. They start with the person they feel emotionally closest to at that moment and place a kiss on their nose. That person then immediately passes on the same display of affection, in the same manner (same place, some volume, passionately or tentatively) to their neighbour.

## Tip

Teenaged sons and daughters need not necessarily be 'spared' this game, because often these stroppy teenagers are precisely the ones who are in need of such gestures. And, once they get used to the game, they will lose their dread of touch.

# The Treasure in the Fridge

It is common knowledge that the way to a person's heart is through their stomach.

For this reason it is a good idea to keep something in the fridge in the group common room to be consumed after a particular 'tricky' or tense situation.

This could be a favourite pudding that everyone eats from the same bowl, a platter that is eaten Roman-style while lying on the floor and using fingers, or brightly coloured hard-boiled eggs (regardless of whether or not it is Easter) – there are no limits to group members' imagination.

If group members like they could toast the reconciliation meal with a chant they have thought of together.

# Guessing Massage

It doesn't matter whether someone is annoying bickerer or a permanent sourpuss, today they are going to have the pleasure of a guessing massage.

For this, the person lies on their stomach or their side in the middle of the floor. This can be made more comfortable by having a towel to lie on, with a small cushion for the head. Then they are covered with a soft blanket and asked to close their eyes. From now on, they are not allowed to peek!

The first masseur creeps up and starts 'massaging' gently through the blanket, using calm circular movements or rhythmical pats and moving up and down the body.

Between movements, the masseur writes, with a finger, the initial of their first name up to three times on the back of the person who is being massaged. Letters should be written as large as possible across the person's back.

Can the person lying down guess who has been massaging them? Having to guess the identity of their masseur is the perfect excuse for having to undergo this massage – and being massaged is a wonderful experience, for people of all ages.

## Note

Make sure everyone is clear that massages should be gentle and ensure those taking part are comfortable with touching.

# Fingers in the Feely Box

Fill a medium –sized box with dried rice, lentils and peas. Cut hand holes in the sides and ask three or four players to use one hand to rummage around in the box and experience the feeling of running their fingers through the cool, dry pulses.

Now encourage them to look out for other fingers. They may automatically pull back or start laughing when they are suddenly touched. Encourage players to continue until everyone knows whose hands they are touching.

## Tip 1

Cover all 'immersed' hands with a cloth so no-one can see where the hands are.

## Tip 2

Foot guessing is also great fun.

## Materials

☀ a box

☀ rice

☀ lentils

☀ peas

# Taking a Deep Breath

Conscious breathing can be an excellent way of calming yourself down. The following relaxation exercise is suitable even for younger children.

The group sit comfortably on chairs. To start with, ask everyone to take one or two deep breaths and breathe out audibly or even 'sing out', which will sound a bit like a siren. Encourage them to start with as high a note as possible and gradually lower their voice right down, while breathing out using a sound sequence they have chosen for among themselves, for example, 'foo', 'hia', 'hi', 'mu' and so on. Vowels at the beginning of sounds are unsuitable, as they will cause participants to push out their breath rather than release it gradually.

This 'siren choir' is likely to sound quite hilarious and make everyone laugh, which is great, because it will make the second part of this exercise even easier. For this, ask the group to place both hands on their stomachs and to breathe in against the weight of their hands, pushing out their stomach.

While doing this, they should count to three before exhaling, again to the count of three.

Repeat this breathing exercise until everyone feels relaxed.

## Tip

If you like, this exercise can also be carried out lying down.

# Ca-ter-pil-lar

One person is chosen to be the 'guesser' and is sent outside. Meanwhile, the others quietly decide on a word to be guessed. Divide your group into as many smaller groups as there are syllables in the word. Agree which group is going to say which syllable.

For instance, the word to be guessed is 'caterpillar'. The strange concert begins as soon as the guesser re-enters the room: The first group shouts rhythmically 'Ca, ca, ca', the second group 'ter, ter, ter', the third group 'pil, pil, pil' and the last group 'lar, lar, lar'.

Everyone should call out at the same time and in the same rhythm to try to confuse the poor guesser. If they manage to work out the word, they can choose the next person to be the guesser.

# Fan Ball

For this game each person needs a table tennis ball and a wide object to fan with, such as a piece of cardboard or a paper plate.

Using pieces of string, mark the start and finish of a 'fanning track'. Several players start at the same time by placing their table tennis balls on the starting line. As soon as the start signal is given players have to try to move their balls along the track and across the finish line by fanning them with their paper plates. They are not allowed to touch their balls with their plates. The winner is the first person to fan their ball across the finish line.

## Tip

This game can be made more difficult by introducing some obstacles to move around or through (for example, an empty cardboard roll).

## Materials

☼ table tennis balls

☼ paper plates or strips of cardboard

☼ string

# Nature Mandalas

A mandala is a term for a symbolic diagram, usually a circle enclosing a square and other patterns, that represents the universe and which is used within different religions, including Hinduism and Buddhism. The psychologist C. G. Jung viewed the term as a symbol of the self, or the soul, representing wholeness and unity in the shape of a circle or square.

This activity requires group members to work together to come up with a plan for an unusual mandala – made completely from natural materials.

First, group members draw different patterns on a large piece of paper and note down ideas of materials to be used.

Afterwards everyone goes out to look for the natural materials, these can be pebbles, leaves, twigs, fruits, seeds, etc. Obviously, if anyone comes across something particularly interesting or unusual, they should bring that back.

Once all the materials have been collected, the group can reproduce their plan as a model on the floor or on a table. Flowers, conkers, grasses, beechnuts, leaves and pebbles should be arranged carefully to create a colourful and completely natural mandala.

## Tip

Don't forget your camera!

## Materials

☼ large piece of paper

☼ natural materials

# Pin the Tail on the ....

Draw an animal on a large piece of paper – any animal can be chosen, as long as it has a tail. However, the animal's tail is not actually drawn, as the players will be taking it in turns to stick a tail made of string on to the picture.

This task is made more difficult by blindfolding the player whose turn it is to pin the tail on the animal. All that players have to rely on is their instinct and memory: Where approximately might the elephant's bottom be?

## Rules

☀ If a player misses the animal altogether, they get no points.

☀ If the player sticks the tail anywhere on the animal's body, they get one point.

☀ Three points are awarded if a player manages to stick the tail on the right end of the body.

☀ The winner, with five points, is the player whose tail is closest to the correct place.

## Tip

If using one tail each, make sure to label everyone's tail before the beginning of the game.

## Materials

☀ large sheets of paper

☀ pens

☀ pieces of string or wool

# Soap Operas

In this game two groups will put their sleight of hand and ability to react quickly to the test. Divide into two teams of equal number, each team should form a circle and choose a 'soap master'.

The soap master stands in the middle of the circle and is in charge of a new piece of soap and a bucket of lukewarm water. At a signal, the soap master briefly dunks the soap into the water and then squeezes the soap with both hands so it jumps in the direction of one of the players in the circle. If that player manages to catch the soap, their group is given one point.

Another point is given if the catcher is able to return the soap in the same way and the soap master manages to catch it again. Play continues this way until everyone has had a turn. If the soap is dropped, no points are given.

Instead of playing for points, teams could compete for the quickest time. The first group to complete the round wins.

If the soap is dropped, that throw has to be repeated until the person has caught it before the round can continue.

## Tip

Soap operas work best outside, especially when it is sunny and everyone is wearing swimming costumes!

## Materials

☼ pieces of soap

☼ bucket

# Knot Race

Two courses are marked out on a field by placing 10 to 20 coloured cones, sticks or fur cones at regular intervals.

Two teams line up. The first runner from each team is given a knotted cloth or other easily carried object.

At the start signal they must run up to the first marker, put down the knotted cloth and continue running to the last marker, turning around and running back to the beginning where they start off the second player by touching their out-stretched hand.

The second player runs off, picks up the cloth at the first marker and moves it to the second marker before running to the end, turning round and running back again to touch hands with the third person, who has to pick up the knot and move it to the third marker, and so on.

If players are particularly fit, the teams can return the knot, marker by marker, to the beginning of the course.

The group who completes the course first, and with each person placing the knot by the correct marker, is the winner.

## Materials

☼ course markers (e.g., cones or sticks)

☼ cloth

# Richard's VIP Club

In order to become a member of the VIP Club, players have to meet certain requirements. They must work out what Richard likes and what he doesn't . An insider can provide some examples:

☀ Richard loves riding, but not swimming.

☀ Richard loves radishes, but not broccoli.

☀ Richard loves running, but not cycling.

Players then take turns to name things that might meet Richard's taste. Anyone who has worked out the system is allowed to join this exclusive club and can start to think of new requirements for the next round.

The answer is:
Richard only likes things beginning with R and is not interested in anything else.

## Further ideas

Rob's club only likes things containing double letters.
Sophie's club prefers things containing the vowel 'o'.

# Indicators

This indicator game requires a lot of concentration and is great fun!

The players sit in a circle. The first person to start puts their hands by the sides of their head, with their thumbs touching their temples. Their fingers are then used as indicators by rotating the wrists.

The person who starts uses their hands to contact another player in the circle. Everyone must pay attention so they don't miss the signal, to reinforce the indicators, players can also wink with their eyes.

The person who has been contacted by indicator must react quickly by returning the message with their own hands. In addition, the person on their right has to join in by indicating with their left hand while the person on their left has to indicate with their right hand.

Only when all three are indicating is the first person allowed to stop. The receiver must now indicate at someone else in the circle. With the exception of the first player, there will always be three players in motion.

# Cuckoo in the Nest

All players sit next to each other on chairs in a semi-circle. Opposite the group, sitting on the floor, is the 'cuckoo', holding a stock of folded pieces of paper with numbers on them, one for each player. Each number occurs twice, so two players will get the same number. These are handed out, one to each person in the group.

All players must keep their numbers secret. It is important that the cuckoo does not find out anybody's number, because they must discover who has which number which they do by calling out a number, for example, '2'.

As those with number 2 will have no clue who the other person with number 2 is, the two of them will have try to communicate using eye contact and body language without attracting the cuckoo's attention. Once they have found each other they must quickly try to swap places. The cuckoo's task is to try to sit in one of their places. If the cuckoo manages to reach one of the chairs before a number 2 can sit down, the cuckoo can stay there and the chairless player becomes the new cuckoo.

After a few rounds, the number partners will all know each other and conquering the nest will become a matter of concentration and running speed.

## Tip

The game can be made more difficult if the cuckoo calls out two different numbers to swap places.

# Treat Ludo

This delicious variation of the traditional Ludo game uses four different types of healthy treats instead of the usual counters, for example, four raisins, four crackers, four grapes, and so on.

Players follow the rules of the conventional Ludo game on a standard board. As soon as someone has thrown a six, they can start off one of their healthy counters. There is only one point where the rules differ from usual: if an enemy cracker lands on the same space as a raisin, the raisin is not sent back to the start, but is eaten by the enemy cracker player.

Patience will be put to the test as players watch their counters being eaten before they make it to the finish and you might, therefore, want to allow for an emergency supply of counters!

The group could also make their own game boards, whose appearance matches the healthy counters. This could be laminated and used for further games.

# The Old King is Ill

The group sits in a circle. One player is appointed to be the first king's general – each person will have a turn as the round progresses - and announces:

'The old, old king is ill!'

The other players respond in unison:

'What is – what is – what is wrong with him?'

The general responds immediately:

'His left eye is twitching.'

All players start to twitch frantically with their left eyes until another general announces a second message from the palace:

'The old, old king is ill!'

'What is – what is – what is wrong with him?'

'His teeth are chattering!'

As the round progresses, the king suffers from more and more ailments. And what's more, he is suffering from them all at the same time!

The challenge for the group is to act out all these ailments simultaneously without bursting out laughing at the same time.

# Messy Forfeits

When the house or classroom looks like an untidy tip, it is time for 'Messy Forfeits'.

Suddenly, and without allowing any excuses, the game is announced. As quickly as possible all group members have to rush to collect any objects that are lying around and put them into a basket or box. Then the basket is covered with a cloth and placed on the table. The tension will rise as the group leader reaches under the cloth and, without revealing the object, asks 'What kind of messy forfeit should be carried out by the owner of this object?'

The group then suggest different forfeits from which the leader selects one. Now the object is revealed – it is brought out of the basket revealing the identity of its owner, who must give in to their fate and carry out the forfeit.

This could be, for example, reciting the 17-times table backwards or doing a Cossack dance. The forfeit is only complete when the tell-tale object has been appropriately tidied up or put away.

The game continues until all items in the basket have been tidied away.

# Chore Snap

To prepare for this game, the group members draw symbols representing different tidying-up chores onto small cardboard squares (approx 8cm x 8cm).

*For example:*

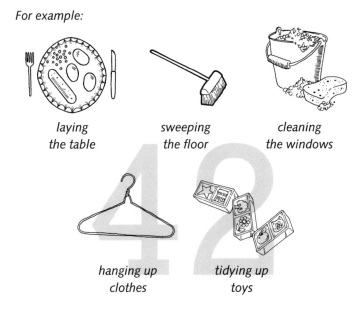

laying
the table

sweeping
the floor

cleaning
the windows

hanging up
clothes

tidying up
toys

Each symbol card has an identical partner. The group must create as many cards as are needed (simply divide the number of chores to be done by the number of group members).

At the beginning of the week, group members get together, shuffle the picture cards and place them face-down on the table. Then they play Chore Snap.

Players take turns to turn over a picture card. Once turned over, cards remain face-up on the table. As soon as someone turns over a card that matches one that is already visible, that player calls out 'Snap' and is allowed to keep the picture pair. The player is now responsible for the chore illustrated on the cards for the remainder of the week.

As it would be unfair for one person to have more chores than anyone else, either people can stop once they have a certain number of cards, or you can compare how many cards each person has at the end of the game. The extra cards can be shared out until everyone has approximately the same number of chores for the week.

This game is great for highlighting the many chores that have to be done during a normal week and provides a fun way for people to develop their sense of responsibility within the group.

## Materials

- ☼ cardboard
- ☼ scissors
- ☼ pens

# Roll and Clear the Table

When everyone is sitting around with full stomachs after a delicious meal and no one seems to be able to summon up enough energy to start clearing the table, it is time to play 'Roll and Clear the Table'.

A dice makes its way round the group and each player is allowed to roll it just once. The number on the dice indicates how many pieces of crockery or cutlery a player has to clear from the table.

This method can also be used for clearing up classrooms and group spaces.

# Leave it to Chance

When you are trying to find someone to do an everyday 'job' that no one really wants to do, for example, cleaning out the fish tank, tidying up the toys or helping in the kitchen, you can leave it to 'chance' to decide who is going to do the job.

One player is appointed to be 'Chance' and, equipped with a whistle, leaves the room or turns away so they cannot see the others.

The other group members arrange themselves in a circle. An object representing the job to be done is then passed around the circle in a clockwise direction. 'Chance' starts the game by blowing the whistle from outside the room and one player starts by passing the object to their neighbour. Everyone will try to pass the object on to the next person as quickly as possible because they know that, as soon as the whistle is blown for the second time, the person who is holding the object at that time has 'won' the job.

As a small consolation prize that person is then appointed to be 'Chance' while the next job is being assigned and, for that round at least, does not have to worry about being given another job to do.

## Materials

☼ whistle

☼ objects representing different chores

# Beer Mats Puzzle

For this game, group members have to collect some beer mats or postcards, preferably all with the same picture.

To play the game, each player has some of the beer mats or postcards in front of them. Using a felt tip pen, but without using a ruler, they must draw a creative line dividing the mat or card into two halves. It doesn't matter whether the line goes from corner to corner or from side to side, or whether it is curved or a zig-zag. Now they must use scissors to cut along their lines and end up with two puzzle pieces for each beer mat or postcard.

Now the game can start. The card or mat halves are shuffled and spread out on the table. One player starts by choosing one of the halves and is given two minutes to try to find its matching other half. Once the two minutes are over, the pieces are shuffled once more and it is the next player's turn.

## Variation

All group members play at the same time, rummaging through the pile of beer mat halves. The winner is the player who gets the most matching pairs at a set time.

# Nutolini

Be aware of any possible nut allergies before playing this game.

All players sit around a table. In the middle of the table there is a large bowl containing equal numbers of a selection of different nuts such as walnuts, brazil nuts and hazelnuts.

The player who is going to start is blindfolded and puts on a thin pair of gloves. Then the blindfolded player starts rummaging around in the bowl of nuts, feeling the different shapes and chooses one type of nut. Their challenge is to find all nuts of this type without looking.

One point is given for each correct nut. The number of wrong nuts is taken off the points given for the correct nuts and the total is noted down on a piece of paper. Then it is the next player's turn.

## Materials

☼ bowl

☼ different types of nuts

☼ paper

☼ pen

# Fruit Battleships

For this game, each player needs to have two pieces of A4 squared paper, which is divided into 16 squares of equal size using a black pen. To cut down on work, one piece of paper can be prepared and then photocopied for the group.

Group members play in pairs, and each person is given two pieces of paper. To start with, each player draws an apple, a pear, cherries, a banana and a pineapple in any of the squares on one piece of paper, keeping each piece of fruit within a square. Encourage them to cover their pieces of paper to hide from their partners where they are placing their fruit.

At a signal, players swap pieces of paper and are allowed to look at their partner's plan for 30 seconds. Ask them to really concentrate and try to memorise where on the page their partner has drawn the different pieces of fruit. Then players swap back and, from memory, try to draw their partner's fruit into the correct empty squares on their second piece of paper.

Afterwards, partners can evaluate how well they have done. Two points can be given for each correct piece of fruit in the correct square, one point is given for a wrong piece of fruit in the right square.

## More difficult variation

To make the game more difficult you could either increase the number of squares on the plan or get players to draw more pieces of fruit, or even do both.

## Tip

You could mark the squares with numbers or symbols to facilitate visual memory.

# Clover Leaf

'Clover Leaf' is a fun organisation game played under timed conditions.

Each player is given a piece of paper and a pen and awaits instructions from the group leader. For example, players are asked to draw four-leaf clovers containing four different symbols. The first leaf of the clover might have a red circle on it, the second a blue square, the third a yellow coloured-in sun and the fourth green leaf veins.

Each player arranges the required colours in front of them and waits for the signal to start drawing. How many correctly completed four-leaf clovers did the fastest player manage to draw in the given time?

## Tip

If you want to avoid scruffily drawn clover leaves, you might want to consider preparing some photocopied outlines of four-leaf clovers.

# Cuckoo

This game is about finding the odd one out, the 'cuckoo in the nest'!

An overhead projector or board is used to show five words or objects at a time, which have one thing in common. For example:

☀ They are edible.

☀ They are used for transport.

☀ They can swim.

However, there is a 'cuckoo' amongst the five words that does not really belong to that category. Who can find it first?

## Examples

☀ Tram, train, car, roller skates, aeroplane

☀ Crab, fish, boat, surfboard, kite

☀ Oats, wheat, potatoes, rye, barley

This game can be used to encourage children to be more focused and pay more attention to the content of conversations, as they will learn that something can be categorised differently depending on criteria and context.

# Line Salad

A 'line salad' can be created by using a dark pen to draw circles, loops, snaked lines, squiggles and so on a large piece of light-coloured paper.

Members of the group are then asked to find some kind of order in the maze of lines by looking for structures or pictures that might have been created by chance within the drawing. Any details or designs found can be carefully traced over and coloured in with colouring pens. Even if players cannot find any specific shapes, they are still likely to be able to find lots of patterns to colour in.

## Tip

This game is also fun when two players sit opposite each other working on the same 'line salad'.

*Have you seen ...*

# 3 Minute Motivators

*More Than 120 Activities to Help you Reach, Teach and Achieve!*

Kathy Paterson

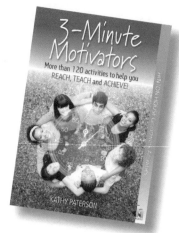

This resource will show you how to turn around unmotivated, unfocused classes. With more than 120 practical and simple ideas that will refocus a group, release excess energy, or start a class with a bang.

Offering a wide variety of ready-to-use activities that turn potential problems into opportunities, and get pupils out of a rut and into a more productive mode:

- *Calm Down* – relaxing activities that let imaginations soar

- *Get Moving* – lively motivators

- *Act, Don't Speak* – silent but fun activities

- *Words and Movement* – activities that mix talk with action

- *Single Words & Sounds* – simple communication activities

- *Conversation* – getting motivated one-on-one

- *Brainstorms* – working together to let the ideas fly

- *Paper & pencil activities* – from letter and word play to shared stories.

An ideal resource for all teachers, teaching assistants and those running groups, promoting playful activities that involve competition, cooperation and opportunities to focus on real learning.

*2009 • 168pp • photocopiable A4 paperback • 978-1-906531-00-3*

**Hinton House Publishers Ltd**
Newman House, 4 High Street, Buckingham, MK18 1NT, UK
info@hintonpublishers.com
www.hintonpublishers.com

# The 50 Best Games series ...

☼: These handy pocket books will ensure you are never again stuck for activity ideas that will help make both teaching and learning fun!

☼: Carefully selected, each collection of the 50 Best Games is themed and addresses a specific area of development. All the games are easy to implement with the minimum of preparation and can be adapted to the needs of your particular group.

☼: Use them as warm-ups, ice breakers, time fillers or to address a specific need. Suitable for groups of all sizes and can be used with all ages from young children to adolescents.

**The 50 Best Games for Building Self-Esteem**

ISBN 978-0-906531-18-8

**The 50 Best Games for Sensory Perception**

ISBN 978-0-906531-11-9

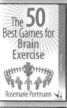

**The 50 Best Games for Brain Exercise**

ISBN 978-0-906531-14-0

**The 50 Best Games for Relaxation & Concentration**

ISBN 978-0-906531-17-1

**The 50 Best Games for Speech & Language Development**

ISBN 978-0-906531-13-3

**The 50 Best Games for Children's Groups**

ISBN 978-0-906531-12-6

**The 50 Best Games for Groups**

ISBN 978-0-906531-16-4

**The 50 Best Indoor Games for Groups**

ISBN 978-0-906531-15-7

**Hinton House Publishers Ltd**
Newman House, 4 High Street, Buckingham, MK18 1NT, UK
info@hintonpublishers.com
www.hintonpublishers.com